Lee's Corner
VOL. II

Copyright ©2020 by Lee Hulsey

All rights reserved

This is a work of fiction. Any resemblance to actual places or events or persons, living or dead, is purely coincidental.

All rights reserved. No part of this book may be reproduced or transmitted in any form or by any means, electronic or mechanical, including photocopying, recording, or by any information storage and retrieval system, without permission in writing from the Author or Author's family.

Synopsis of Lee-ism's

I would rather think of my Golden Nuggets as a thought process, a relatively short narrative with a more or less complex idea, about human beings, their feelings, thoughts, actions, etc.

It is the best and worst, happiest and saddest moments of one's life to stop and think. To absorb a Golden Nugget and pass it on or just cherish it knowing it's there.

There is room for all values in thoughts. Like music, there is Classical, Jazz, Rock and Roll and Alternative. So to critics, it is a matter of taste. Some weeds are beautiful.

I believe my book of Lee-ism's can inspire and motivate the reader to stop and think. It is written for young and old. Readers can relate to the Golden Nuggets – they will touch your heart, and make your spirit sing. Some will give you hope, and some will maybe change your life.

Some are for laughter to show we are all humans and not perfect, and we can laugh at ourselves.

About the Author

Lee Hulsey is a very young 86 year old business woman. She lived in Las Vegas, NV for 45 years and in Fallbrook, CA since 1985.

Lee and her husband, Joe Hulsey, are the owners of Roseland Nurseries in Fallbrook dealing in wholesale and retail. They have been married 67 years! They are so proud of their family which includes 4 sons, 7 grandchildren and 2 great grandchildren!!!

Lee has many experiences in her lifetime, so she is putting those on paper as poems and short stories. She has been published many times. Lee says, "Poetry is one of the best tools for truth. It is the doctor for loneliness, broken hearts and lost dreams." God will help you through the storms, but you have to row the boat. Life is a journey and family is what life is.

Lee loves family first, dancing, fishing, writing and, of course, trees and flowers.

Dedication

"Lee's Corner Volume II" is dedicated to the unsung magnificence of ordinary people.

My family inspired me to keep writing! Kelly & Evanna Hulsey, entrepreneurs of the half century in their own right. My family that was held captive every night on the phone listening to the poems of the day. They were so patient with me. Mike, Tony, Kelly Hulsey. Sisters, Bea Caracciolo and Dee Johnson. Brother, Chester Beene. My best friends; Donna Kramer, Jeanne Rosetta, Mary Gennero, Beti Romero, Azuré Romero. Most of all to God, who woke me every night to write more.

To have passed through this world is an honor! Over a period of three years it took for a time like this!

Thank You!

Great People

SPECIAL THANKS

To Mark Walters, Genco Printers, for your patience and creativity for this book. To Michele Howard at Village News for her enthusiasm and integrity. To Julie Reeder at Village News, the best little newspaper in the U.S.A., for her knowledge and time to help and support. To Samantha Gorman for her creativity and kindness to do this project. To my girl Friday, Azuré Romero, thanks for your excellence in computer programming and helping to organize the second volume of "Lee's Corner."

– Lee Hulsey 2020

Compassion

In compassion there is not one shred
of self pity!
It comes from the complete soul!
Therefore you cannot doubt there
is a soul!!

Hair Day

No hair day is worse than a *bad*
hair day.
Be grateful and love your hair!

The Best Love

The best love is the first love if you can remember it.

Illness

There are many things we can control that make us less vulnerable to illness, none of them come in a pill!!

Teach Love

Teach only love!
For that is what you are.

Love & Peace

Declare love over every situation
and peace will come, every time.

Strongest Love

Who would die for you?
It is the strongest love of all!
Do you have a puppy?

Love

Love talked about can easily
be turned aside.
Love demonstrated will always
abide!

Anchor

Love is the anchor
of the soul!

Precious Possession

A compliment from the one you love is your most precious possession!

Worthy

Let me be worthy of
your love and respect!

Love is Light

Be a conduit of love!
Be a conduit of light!
Evil is darkness.
Love is light.

Power to Feel

Don't give anybody your power to feel!
Sometimes we give away what we love the most, peace!

Innocent

Look at the world as a child.
Everyone is innocent!

Has Been

It's better to have been a *has been* than not been at all!
They have all the fun, so what could be wrong?

Starbucks

If you can't dream it, you can't do it!
Someone dreamed up Starbucks!
Who would think you can make a living selling coffee?

God is Love

God opened up the universe and love came through.
That is the key of life, God is love!

Never Give Up

Live in the present today! But plant seeds of hope for the future tomorrow, never give up! Fill your soul with love and hope.

Ultimate Evil

The ultimate evil is the
absence of love!

God's Love & Guidance

With God's love and guidance
we can do anything!
Make divine appointments
with God and ask!

Success

Success is when preparation meets opportunity and marries!

The Great Mechanic

If your head and body is out of alignment, take it to God. The Great Mechanic! God will align your heart with kindness, forgiveness, compassion, love and you will prosper!

Choose

You can be happy or miserable!
But you can't be both!
What do you choose?

Eighty-Six

Forty years plus forty six years makes me an expert! You can say I'm all the beautiful words! I have a great resume!

Elevate & Propel

God is the one that will elevate you and propel you along your own path so that you may contribute the results of all your lessons to the rest of the world!

Happiness

Happiness is not a search!
It is a decision!
Decide to be happy!

Ignorance

Only ignorance can be influenced.
Where there is true intelligence
There is no influence!

God of Justice

God is a God of justice!
Stop being unhappy with
what someone else is doing
Your will, will be done!

Grudge

Don't waste time carrying a grudge! It's like a bail of hay on your back. It's too heavy to carry on the battlefield. Pick your battles. Some people will never like you.

A Being

We are a being! Being human!

Being Right

It is petty, boring, and monotonous to be right all the time.

Somebody has to be wrong sometimes.

That's a why! Why?

"But"

"But" cancels everything! Don't say, "I love you, but."

Time

What flies by you and
you can't see it?
It's time! Time! Time!

Buttons

You have two buttons to push
in life!
One is up for feeling good!
One is down for feeling bad!
Associate with people that push
your buttons up!

Masterpiece

Run your own race!
God says you are a masterpiece!

Short & Long Memory

I'm just saying!
Talking about baggage, have a short memory for your mistake and bad things.
Have a long memory for all your accomplishments and good things.

Ditch The Baggage

Ditch the baggage! Life is too short to carry around all that heavy stuff. You pay and pay for other baggage, and nobody cares!

Leave Me Alone

When I come back or if I come back I want to be my husband, so I can leave me alone!

Stream of Life

We are all the same in this world! Traveling down the stream of life. Swimming up stream or down stream. Your choice!

Break A Habit

You can't break a habit! You have to replace it!

Be an Eagle

To be an eagle takes great courage! You can be an eagle. Many times in life! That is a hero.

"Sorry"

When you shoot off your mouth and say hurtful, nasty, negative things to someone and you are "sorry,"

You apologize to them but they are still shot!

Not Perfect

We are not perfect and God did not intend for us to be perfect. Only to do our very best, to do the best we can! God loves us as we are, just the same.

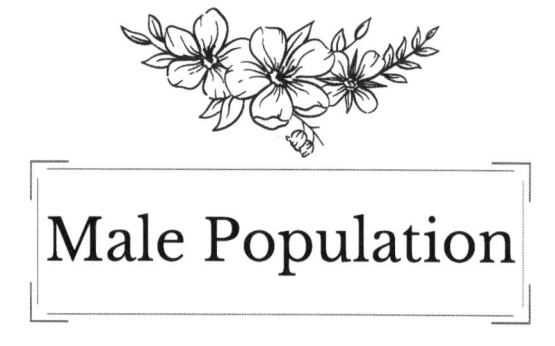

Male Population

Be careful how we talk about the male population! Remember, they gave us a rib so don't make them mad. They may take it back. I'm just saying!

Effort to Change

Don't whine about things you don't make an effort to change. Or, worry about things you cannot change. If you can change it, change it! If you can't change it, forget about it! Next!

Law of The Universe

You never get by getting,
you only get by giving!
Law of the universe.

Mama Said

Mama said, "You can do anything you want to do in this world, you just haven't done it yet!"
And you know she was right!

Love Thy Neighbor

Love thy neighbor.
Real love has to include complete and total concern for the other person without regard to one's own feelings.

Number One

The most important in marriage is "Love your neighbor" as yourself, your spouse is your number one "Neighbor."

Skeletons

An ungodly man or woman digs up "evil."

We all collect skeletons!

Let the matter rest!

Right or Wrong

We need to have moral courage to stand up and do what is right.
Right or Wrong.
What do you choose?
Stand up for the flag!

Pit of Depression

If you are in a deep pit of depression, get a dose of laughter into the sunshine and be grateful for all the good in your life!

Your Choice

Don't critique others to find all their faults to make you feel better! Do the opposite, which makes you feel you are helping others to greatness! Your Choice!

Luke 7:4-7

Her sins, which are many are forgiven for she loved much! But to whom little is forgiven, the same love is little.
- Luke 7:4-7

Philemon

Breaking News
Read Philemon 1 10-17
What an enlightenment!
How brothers should behave!

I Corinthians 13

Love bears all things!
Believes all things!
Endures all things!
Love never ends!
- I Corinthians 13

Friends & Family

We are not alone in this journey.
God provides exactly what we need
first when we need it!
He blessed us with friends
and family.
A simple card or phone call means
so much to someone,
many someone's!
It doesn't cost much and it might be
the most important thing you
ever do!

Song

When you are born, you are born with a song in your heart! Once you find your unique song, nothing and no one can keep you from singing it clearly!

"Hoarder"

There needs to be a "hoarder" rehab for collectors with a twelve step program.
Rule #1 Do I need it? or Do I want it?

A Woman

I'm just saying! A woman needs many projects in her lifetime. So she has a husband and many children, so she will be guaranteed to be a very occupied person the rest of her life!

Currency of Power

Language is the currency of power!

Change

About marriage, always bear in mind that the standards and concepts produced by your parents could be wrong!
There may be another way of doing it. Remember change is a natural way of life! Change is good!

Preparation

Preparation is your currency for opportunity!

A Good Marriage

The most important key to a good marriage is maturity! Love grows with maturity! Selfishness will end a marriage quickly, guaranteed!

100 Percent

Marriage is 100% 100% Marriage is not 50/50.

Hero

Do not tell your wife she doesn't have a job, she doesn't work!
Let's be real!
Your wife and mother has the hardest job God ever created.
Bar none!
She is more than a C.E.O. of the home. She is a wife, mother, friend, confidant, servant, cook, chauffeur, nurse, doctor, organizer, referee, teacher, party planner, psychiatrist. Most of all, she is a Hero! She is admired and has great courage!

The Great Life

When we are born we begin the greatest marathon of life! We do not set the course. The race of life demands that we do away with everything that hinders or threatens our belief in God. Our race requires strength and endurance. It requires love, patience, forgiveness and faith! Stay the course. Remain faithful to the end and we will have lived a great life!

Mental Abuse

Disapproval is a more vicious way of inflicting punishment upon another human being than physical abuse. That is called *mental abuse*! Approval should be expressed both publicly, to assure your friends that you love your partner!

Compliments

People respond more to compliments than condemnation!

Wrong Turn

If you take the wrong turn in life and you get lost, it may be a blessing in disguise. Enjoy the scenery and new beauty and relax!

Dignity

Treat your partner with dignity. A state of being worthy and honored and they will be your partner for life!

Secret of Life

Claiming and realizing God's presence is the secret of life and that secret will open any door, bridge, gaps, remove any obstacle, retrieve any mistake, shut out any sin and clear up any grief.

Don't Go

When things in life go bad, don't go with them!

Saving

Our purpose is to save that which was lost! How are we doing? You can't save it unless you know what it is!

"D"

Take evil and put a "D" in front. What do you get? Ponder this!

Recognize Your Soul

Everything changes when you recognize your soul. It is that big, it is all of you!

Desire

Any good in your life that you desire, you must first build it into your dreams and consciousness. No one can take that from you!

Inside Out

No man or woman has ever been destroyed from the outside! It is from the inside out!

True Image

Nothing can permanently deny its own nature and we surround ourselves with the true image of ourselves.

Change the Inner

If you want peace, harmony, love, abundance and health in your life, you must begin by changing the inner.
The way to do that is to believe God is working through you!

Fear Kills

Fear kills more dreams than failures!

Voice of an Eagle

The foremost responsibility of an eagle scout is to live with honor. Honor is the foundation of all character. An eagle is a hero! Do you know one?

Victim

Don't be a victim!
Love, be nice and get even!

Eagle Scout

An eagle scout is loyal. Without loyalty all character lacks direction! An eagle is loyal to his ideals. An eagle is loyal to his family, friends and his community.

Believe

As you believe, so do you express!

Calm & Focused

Don't get mad or angry or you will lose the game!

Be calm, focused and get even!

One Track Mind

We are all born with a million tracks in the brain. Why have a "one track mind?" We only use 5% of the tracks!

Wonder

I wonder why I wonder?
I'm wondering what you are wondering
I wonder if you like me?
I wonder if you love me?
I wonder if its gonna rain?
I wonder if you're going to call?
Wonder! Wonder! Wonder!

Stop Thinking

Stop thinking!
Start feeling good!

Dicker

It's great to Dicker! Are you a dickerer or do you pay full price?
Dicker, Dicker, Dicker!
Everyone loves to dicker! We are all givers, lovers, and pleasers. Why not dicker? What do you have to lose?

Manager

You are your life's manager!
Get it? Be a good manager!

Choices

Life is choices!
Choose to be beautiful!
Choose to be good, kind, honest, and caring!
Choose to give and forgive!
Choose to be happy!
For a wonderful life!

Losing

If you are losing, it means someone else is winning!

Enemies

You need not to fear your enemies! You need not to cast a thought to them, unless it is a good thought, for they are absolutely powerless to hurt you! No one can do that but yourself!

Ignorance Can Kill

You can change what you acknowledge!
Ignorance can kill you.

Destroy

Nothing is ever destroyed from the outside! It can only be destroyed from the inside!

Life Manager

Keep your expectation realistic! Don't be naive.
You can't fire your life manager! So work with it to motivate, educate and be patient with!

Own Client

As your own client you must treat yourself with great care and manage yourself with the understanding that you are a very important person!

Story

Keep your eyes and ears open. Everyone has a story to tell. Don't miss it! It might be the best thing you ever hear!

The Game

What gives you the right when you are blessed with talent, training, a healthy body, and such a vibrant mind to check out of the game called life?

Fear Not

Jesus said, "fear not" 365 times in the bible.
If you don't believe that read the bible and count them!

The Right

You don't have the right to hide behind fear. You don't have the right to waste your gifts. You are cheating yourself and everyone whose life you could be blessing!

Good Tenants

Don't let anyone rent a space in your head unless they are good tenants!

"'Sold Out"

You can lie here and whine and let the scum of the earth own you for the rest of your life or you can get off your butt and go after your dreams! You must decide that your dreams are not "sold out." You are worth the risk!

Book

You cannot judge a book by the cover!

The Bear

The bear said, "If you could read my mind, you would back away slowly and run for your life!"

Delay Judgment

Delaying judgement can help you avoid prejudices and give you time to employ higher principles, such as gratitude and compassion to guide your actions.

Monday

Monday: Gratitude
Start your day by finding five things to be thankful for.

Tuesday

Tuesday: Compassion
Have good intentions to ease pain and suffering whenever you can.

Wednesday

Wednesday: Acceptance
Live your day by accepting yourself as you are and others as they are!

Thursday

Thursday: Meaning and Purpose
Focus on the ultimate meaning and purpose of your life. This requires a degree of humility and perspective.

Friday

Friday: Forgiveness
Forgive yourself for past mistakes and then forgive others. You'll have a fresh new start!

Saturday

Saturday: Celebration
Celebrate your life and the lives of those around you! Savor the joy!

Sunday

Sunday: Reflection
Awareness that life is for living!
Pray and meditate.
Be grateful for what you have and share your knowledge to the world!

Great Beauty

Everyday find something beautiful! It's easy, just look around, up or down. Great beauty!

Rule of the Universe

To be successful you have to have many failures first. Isn't that wonderful? It's the rule of the universe!

A Dream

It's only a dream until you write it down. Then, it becomes a goal!

16 Summers

Your kids only have 16 summers with you. Then boy meets girl and the rest is history!

Galatians 5:1

It is for freedom that Christ has set us free! Stand firm and do not let yourself be burdened by a yoke of slavery. Galatians 5:1

"Follow Me"

Remember Jesus said "Follow Me" not the rules of the world on how to live! Live your own life or someone else will live your life for you.

What You Want

How can you have what you want in life if you don't know what you want?

Children Suffer

Children suffer for the
adults ego!
It's very sad when members
of the same family do not
talk with each other.

One Night Stand

I'm just saying, there is no
such thing as a one night
stand. No one is standing.

Three Words

In marriage, leave three words at the alter:
I, Me & Mine
In a successful relationship you may use,
Us, We, & Ours.

Angina

Some people have angina pains. Some people are angina pain!

Do Something

Do Something!
To do nothing at all is
not an option!

Glorious Miracle

Live life as a glorious
miracle not a catastrophe
waiting to happen!

Ten Commandments

Can you name the "Ten Commandments?" The ones you can't remember may be the ones you are guilty of!

Zippidy

My zippidy do dah, doesn't have anymore zippidy yay!

Grandchildren

Grandchildren can always bring you back to reality and show you what is really important in life!

More Than A Smoothie

Life is to be lived and loved!
It is more than a smoothie!

Tears

In marriage, many a tear has to fall. Each tear is a learning game. We can choose to keep smiling or we can go down the drain!

Forgot

I think I forgot something one time! But I can't remember what!

Bitter

Be aware that few things are more bitter than to feel bitter!

Credit Line

Have a good credit line, add to your credits every day. When you need them they will show you your worth!

Gossip

Gossip is a horrible disease!
It is a killer!
It changes lives forever!
Is it true before you say it?
You can never take it back!
No matter the assassination of
character has been done!
In the ruins it leaves behind.
Broken families, dreams, hearts.
Sometimes life imprisons.
Is it worth it?
Your choice!

Self Respect

Never beg someone to be in your life! If your texts, calls, and visits gets ignored, Walk away. It's called self respect! The right people will love you no matter what!

Do & Done

It's great to make a do and a done!

Leave A Trail

Do not follow a path to where it might lead! Instead, go where there is no path and leave a trail!

Positive Energy

Don't waste your time on negative thoughts! Always radiate positive energy!

Resentments

Write down all your resentments and then ask *why?*

Coffee

I drink a lot of water but a lot of it has coffee in it!

Weight

Only put as much weight on your shoulders as you want to carry!

A Cook

"Hello, this is your personal chef." You can't tell a cook by it's cover!

Oyster

You are the oyster
and the pearl!

Ebb and Flow

Ebb & Flow of Life is

Good and Bad

Happy and Sad

Great Accomplishments

Great Failures

Great Defeats

Great Victories

Run The Race

It's not who wins the race,
It's who *runs* the race!

Good Luck

Definition of Good Luck:
Working Hard.

Luckier

The harder you work,
The luckier you are!

Fix it

If your laugh is broken,
Fix it!
It is medicine for the soul.

Auto Pilot

Auto pilot is not our friend,
Walk like you mean it!
Be in control!
Plant your feet,
Hold your head up high and breathe.

Donald Trump

Don't give up,
Be a Donald Trump!

What If

Baby Eagle said to momma eagle as
she was pushed out the nest,
"What if I fall?"
Momma eagle said to baby eagle,
"What if you fly?"
Baby Eagle said,
"Thank you momma."

More

There is more to life
than suffering.

Life of Gratitude

Live a life of gratitude and celebrate your life. You are worthy. It's ok to have a party!

Read A Book

Read a book, you can be anywhere you want to be. Paint a picture of your life! Write a novel. Get a puppy.

Divide Your Love

Your heart beats 38 million times a year!
Make sure it is for the good of the universe!
Don't take up space and oxygen.
Divide your love in life and it will multiply!

Getting & Giving

Who is getting all the getting!
Who is giving all the giving!

No More, No Less

We are not one person!
We are many persons!
Sometimes we are lazy.
Everyday we are different!
We have the "blahs."
We are sad, happy, angry,
depressed, lonely, and
melancholy.
We are a different race.
With a different class in every
race.
No more, no less!

Keeping On

Live, laugh and enjoy life!
Keep on keeping on!
The best is yet to come!

Get A Song

God respects you when you work, but he loves when you sing!
Get a song in your heart so you have something to sing!

Smile

Smile, its free!
It doesn't cost a thing!

Language

Poetry has a language of its own.
Maybe not your language.
Maybe not my language, but a language just the same.
Language of the body, the soul, the heart, and the mind.

Lee-isms

Some Lee-isms may get under your skin, all the way to the core!
They may make you uneasy.
You may be guilty!
Take 3 deep breaths and be understanding!
It's only an opinion.

Think of You

I think of you often!
It doesn't cost a thing!

The Saints

God is not watching the patriots and eagles in the Superbowl 2018. God only watches the saints!

Mama Raised Me

Mama raised me up for a time like this!
Mama said, "It was down the road a piece." Of course she was so right!

Get A Puppy

Your life is not over, until
the fat lady sings
Your life is not over until hell
freezes over
Your life is not over until
Gods willing and the creek
doesn't rise
Your life is not over until you
die
Don't say I'm bored to death!
"Get a puppy"

Love Yourself

I am not your enemy!
You are your enemy,
understand it away.
Love yourself, really love
yourself!
And you will live a happy life!

Lifetime

It's not what you have in your
lifetime,
It's what you do with what you have!

You Are Not

It's not what you are!
The most important is
what you are *not*!

Giant Puzzle

Life is a giant puzzle.
Many pieces don't fit.
And they could never fit so
accept what you can't change.

Willing

You can't say you are willing to try unless you are willing to fail!

Everything

Why is everything you need somewhere else?

Happy Friday

Happy Friday!
Can you feel the love?
Love is everywhere!

Criticize

If you are being criticized,
Go to Jesus,
He will un-criticize you.

Accustomed

Just because you've gotten
accustomed to having a
certain way,
Doesn't mean it's the right way.
Challenge this!
Ponder!

My Illness

My illness could be me,
myself and I!
Ponder this. Could be.

Death

How many close calls of
death have you had?
And made it through
smelling like a rose?
That is God's Angels.

Haste

Haste very slowly!

Bad Habit

You can't break a bad habit.
You can only replace it with
a good habit.. like please!
Thank You!
Your Choice.

Biggest Miracle

The biggest miracle of all
is God made the body!

Our Will

God gave us the heart, soul, and
spirit to live a good life!
Or not!
Our choice, he gives us our will.

Lived A Good Life

To have lived a good life,
You must have in your life,
love, honor, integrity, truth
and most of all God!

Control Freaks

When you get two control freaks
in a room together,
One of them is going to freak out!
I'm just saying, somebody has to
leave the room.

Climb

I'm just saying,
You can't start climbing at the
top of the mountain, you have
to start at the bottom.

Our Forests

You must believe there is a
supreme being,
When you see the sunrise,
When you see the sunset!
How does that appear every day?
Who waters billions of trees in
the forest?
Who takes care of all the billions
of animals?
Thank God for our forests.

The Right Thing

The timing is always right
To do the right thing!

Rise Up

When we are born poor
and ignorant,
We have to rise up from
our "raising."

Saints & Sinners

Our teachers in life are saints and sinners.
We grow and learn from all the fears of childhood which is the mother of depression.

Bucket or Chuck

Bucket it or Chuck it!

Proverbs 11:25

The generous soul will be made rich and he who waters will also be watered himself.
Proverbs 11:25

Grit & Glory

If you're not here for the true grit, you can't be there for the glory.

Light & Sunshine

Truth is the light
and sunshine of life!

Child of God

I am a child of God and a
gentle soul,
but I carry a stick!

No Matter

Walk the talk, no matter
Be a believer, no matter
Hold on, no matter
Hold your head high, no matter
Be peaceful, no matter

Death Is Welcomed

Sometimes death is
welcomed,
and necessary and sad.

Born Free

We are born free,
We put ourselves in prison!

Anger & Hate

Anger masks the fear of dying. Hate is a normal reaction and is handled with maturity. Or not. For our peace we have to accept who we are and whom we are not!

Absolute

You cannot achieve absolute victory, there is no absolute!

Our Mansion

Our mansion of our soul is built out of bricks that others have provided for our growth!

Lonely

We are not isolated so it is unnecessary to be lonely!

Contagious

Every saint and every sinner has been contagious! You have a chance to learn or not.

Limitations

We have limitations, we cannot have all the gifts!
We create life and keep growing!

Accept

Accept that you are not a genius and just live a happy common life!

God's Voice

Let God's voice be louder than the voice of fear.

I Know I Am

I know very little but I know God is all and that is all that matters. I know I am!

Recording

Be careful how you act and talk!
God has a recorder and he is recording you.

Hold On

Be patient, hold on.
It's better to be 6 feet apart than 6 feet under!
Hold on.

Love Lifted Me

Love lifted me!
Love lifted me when nothing would help.
Love lifted me!

Victorious Over Grief

Trust life, face it without a mask or masquerade and you will conquer sorrow and be victorious over grief!

Peaceful Sleep

The more you give, the more peaceful you sleep!

Road Map

Our conscience is our road map to make important decisions. You can never shut it up! It never stops bugging you!
If it's wrong, it lets you know loud and clear.
God is watching.

Unteachable

When someone is unteachable. you have to stop teaching and start praying!

Pay The Dues

We grow up with saints and sinners. We have choices how to live!
At the end we pay the dues, how we live and how we are.

Home

Amazing Grace.
Church is wherever you are!
At work...
At Albertsons...
At Costco...
At Target...
At Home Depot...
Most important at "home."

You Are Free

God said "You are free," you can go to work for me. Thank you God.

Gift To God

Your life is a gift from God.
What you do with your life
is your gift to God!

Truth Wins

Truth always wins,
And is very patient to do so!

Whole Life

Dogs are not your whole life!
But they make your life
whole!

The Right Place

You may be at the right
place at the right time for
a time like this. Amen.

God Gives

God gives us eyes to see,
God gives us ears to hear,
God gives us a voice to talk,
He prepares a path to walk!

Journey

It's not the destination that's important, it's the journey!

Relax & Enjoy

If you get lost living, relax. Enjoy the scenery! You may see something you may have never seen before!

Think

A cat has to meow,
A dog has to bark,
We have to think before we talk!

Marriage

Marriage is a wonderful thing, but you have to work the program!

Get The Job Done

Show me someone that is busy, and I'll show you someone that will get the job done!

Roses

Remember thorns
have roses!

Good Things

Take responsibility for your life.
Take back your power.
Start with small things.
Give yourself credit for the right
things you do.
Focus on the good things!

Guilty

The verdict of guilty
is not for life!

Butterflies

What do butterflies do?
Give us the joy of their
beauty and freedom!

Fisherman

What do you call a woman that loves to fish? Fisherman?

Wagging

Tails wagging are better than tongues wagging!

Guilty & Regret

There is a difference between guilty and regret.

The Facade

As soon as the world knows the lie, the facade, you can start living the truth!

Who You Are

It is not until you find out
who you really are
That you can live a good life.

Treasure

Where is your treasure?
What is your treasure?
Who is your treasure?
What is your vault full of?
What treasures?

Golden Goose

Reach for the Golden Goose. Your going to be thinking anyway. You might as well think great things!

Philodendron

Should I put mayo on my Philodendron plant to make it shine?
Only if you are planning on making a salad.

Seek Love

Do not judge anyone because of gender, color or creed.
Choose to seek love for people not judgement!
Humble yourself.

Change Your Mind

You have to change your mind. God does not change his mind.

What Is Grace?

What is Grace?
Giving to someone love
they do not deserve!

Intimidators

You are never too old or too young to live for Jesus! Walk with the spirit around you. It will blind the intimidators.

Good From Evil

You need to train yourself to distinguish good from evil!

Heart Full

The mouth speaks what is in your heart! What is your heart full of?
Fill it with love.
"True boldness comes from Jesus."

Like A Turtle

Like a turtle, stick
your neck out for a
new venture!

Have An Anchor

In life, it is a long journey!
You have to have an anchor!
You will drift away without an anchor.
Faith is the anchor for the soul!

Stop Evil

You cannot stop evil!
You can only protect
yourself from it or them!

Smug With Success

Don't get smug with "success."
We don't get there alone, ever!
It takes good people helping,
praying, standing tall for you.
Amen.

Drowning

If you are drowning, relax!
You will float.
Fight and you will drown!

The Truth

Jesus says I am the way of the truth!
Know the truth, live, talk,
walk the truth. To know the truth
you will be liberated!
Jesus came to earth for truth!

Stand On The Rock

"I'm just saying"
Your way or the highway?
How, what, when, why?
It could be worse.
When your feelings are hurt stand on the rock! With God at your side.

Fish Out Of Water

You can't live someone else's plan for your life.
You'll be fish out of water.

"Fault Finder"

Don't be a "Fault Finder" unless you open your own closets and clean your own door steps. I'm just saying, there is no perfect!

A Gift

Goodness is a gift from God!
Meanness is a gift from the devil.

Promise

When God makes a promise to us, he keeps it!

Don't ever promise. Instead say I will if God's willing, and the creek doesn't rise.

That's how not to break a heart!

Acquisition Of Knowledge

The acquisition of knowledge is a powerful thing!

Drama Queens

Run fast from passive war mongers. They stand in the back cheering you on with lots of drama. They are called drama queens! No matter the gender. Run fast to stay sane.

Opportunity Presents

When opportunity presents itself, you had better be ready.

Attack Dog

The attack dog cannot change. They are disrespectful, contributing to hurt, fears frustration, intimidation and wanting complete control of your life. Do you know one?

Be Restored

Be restored by asking forgiveness to anyone you have hurt. Demons will tremble!

Contaminated Heart

"I'm just saying"
We have to give to ourselves what we wish we could get from someone else! We have to forgive or we have a contaminated heart!

"Bad Choices"

Don't give power to "bad choices" in your past! Take the power away and they are gone forever!

James 1:4

Let endurance have it's perfect results so that you may be perfect and complete a lacking in nothing.
James 1:4

Extraordinary Life

Only God can help you lead an extraordinary life! Ask and you shall receive.

Higher Power

If you don't have a higher power with you. You will be like a fish out of water!

More Blessings

The more you share in this world, the more blessings shower you every day! Don't lose out because of good intentions.

Gift Of Yourself

Take time to give your greatest gift your time. A gift of yourself!

The Frame

God has you in a frame keeping you safe! Count the times you were saved by the frame. The frame is your protection.

A Better Person

Don't stop getting better! The better you get makes me a better person.

"Dummies"

To be smarter in life, you must associate with people that are smarter than you. Don't hang around "dummies."

Wonderful Things

There is too many beautiful, wonderful things, gifts from God in this world, on this earth to go through it anesthetized.

Time To Live

Ponder this!
We have time to die. But we don't have time to live.
Challenge this with your life!

Blossom

If you are abused or stressed you will never grow and you will never blossom!
Get liberated and free, no matter! So you can blossom as God says to do!

Nursery

A nursery is where money grows on trees!

Alcohol & Drugs

The worm is resentment. The monster is hate, you are feeding it with alcohol and drugs. Reach out to anyone and everyone.

Scorekeeper

Don't be a scorekeeper, there are no winners. Who's counting? God's counting!

Music Zone

I got my feet wet in the music zone. But I never swam with the sharks!

Romans 12:19

Dearly beloved, avenge not yourselves but give peace unto wrath for it is written. Vengeance is mine, saith the Lord, I will repay.
Romans 12:19

American Dream

If you want the American Dream, be the American Dream!

Peacemakers

Blessed are the peacemakers for they shall be called children of God! Peaceful people are powerful people.

Our Legacy

Everything outlasts us on this earth!
Go with the flow. What is, is what is!
We go! Everything else stays behind. Our legacy is the love we leave behind!

Never Stop

"Never Stop Building Your Life"

Pride

Pride comes from pride!
Pride is deceptive.

Song For Chula

You're my buddy, my pal, my
friend and I'll love you till the end,
and I want you to know,
wherever you go!
Your my buddy, my pal, my friend.

Approval

You don't need anyone's approval, only God's approval. Care about people's approval and you will be their prisoner!

One Year

We spend one year of our life looking for lost keys and phones!

No Secret

"It is no secret"
"What God can do"
"What he's done for others"
"He will do for you"
"With arms wide open"
"He will pardon you"
"It is no secret what God can do"

Great Woman

Behind a great man,
there is a great woman.

Spring

Early morning looking East, the sun is coming up and lifting the morning fog.
Yellow butterflies kissing the yellow blossoms on the Acacia Tree.
They are flitting and flirting with each other.
Is this the time to listen and watch?
Hear the quietness of nothing!
So peaceful!
So relaxed!
It must be what love is.

09/06/18
Analisa's Birthday

The Dash

The minister stood to speak, at the funeral of a friend,
He gave the dates on her headstone, from the beginning... to the end.
He mentioned first the date of birth, his eyes welled up in tears, but he said what mattered most of all, was the dash between those years.
For that dash represents all the time, that she lived upon this earth, and now only those who loved her, know what that little line is worth.
For it matters not, how much we own, the cars, the house, the cash. What matters most is how we live, and love,

and how we spend our dash.
So think about this life you've led, are there things you'd like to change?
For life is but a vapor in time, are you at the dash mid-range?
If we could just slow down enough, and consider what's true and real, and take the time to understand, just how other people feel.
And be less quick to anger, and show appreciation more, and love the people in our lives, like we've never loved before.
To treat each other with respect and more often wear a smile, remembering that this special dash lasts for just a little while.
So when your Eulogy is being read, with your life's actions to rehash
Would you be pleased with the things they say, and how you lived your dash?

Office Hours

Open most days about 9 or 10.
Occasionally as early as 7.
But some days as late as 12 or 1.
We close about 5:30 or 6.
Occasionally about 4 or 5.
But some days or afternoons we aren't here at all!
If the fish are biting, we are closed!
Lately we are never here!
We are out to lunch!!

How To De-Stress

1. Thou shalt live in the here and now!
2. Thou shalt not hurry!
3. Thou shalt not take thy self too seriously!
4. Thou shalt always be grateful!

COVID-19

Stop biting your nails. You could get COVID-19. You can't even put your fingers on your face, eyes or mouth. Get it? Stop!

Dear Nurse

What do you see caregiver... what do you see?
What are you thinking... when you're looking at me. A cranky old woman... not very wise?
Uncertain of habit with faraway eyes?
Who dribbles her food and makes no reply.
When you say in a loud voice I wish you'd try!
Who seems not to notice the things that do and forever is losing a sock or a shoe.
Do you see me now? Do you see me then? A beautiful lady and where I have been?

I was a good daughter like you.
I came up poor without a clue! And I was a mother of four!
Do you see a great life lived?
With many grandchildren and greats to come before I go!
One time long ago, I was a beauty like you.
Can you see my life legacy?
I was always kind and loved so many!
I was a caregiver like you to my best friend, my brother, my sister, my son, my husband,
I never forsake them.
Can you see the love?

Senior Dance Camp

When COVID gets out of here, we need a senior dance camp. Could be singles or couples. A nice vacation, just dance, day and night, so much fun!
Worth a million!
Parents need a vacation too!
Sorta like time shares!

Lick & A Promise

Do it a lick and a promise and do it better next time!

Ten Foods For The Brain

1. Olive Oil
2. Avocados
3. Blueberries
4. Dark Chocolate
5. Eggs
6. Grass Fed Beef
7. Dark Green Veggies
8. Broccoli
9. Wild Salmon
10. Almonds

Most Wonderful Book

The most wonderful book ever written is the Bible! The 2nd most wonderful book ever written is The Webster's Large Print Dictionary.
Everyone should read both of these!
Love, Love, Love!

Index Alphabetical

100 Percent 39	Biggest Miracle 100
16 Summers 67	Bitter 75
A Being 21	Blossom 147
A Better Person 145	Book 60
Absolute 110	Born Free 109
Accept 112	Break A Habit 26
Accustomed 98	Bucket or Chuck 105
A Cook 80	But 22
Acquisition of Knowledge 138	Butterflies 125
A Dream 66	Buttons 23
A Gift 137	Calm & Focused 51
A Good Marriage 39	Change 38
Alcohol & Drugs 148	Change the Inner 48
American Dream 150	Change Your Mind 130
Anchor 11	Child of God 107
Anger & Hate 109	Children Suffer 71
Angina 70	Choices 54
Approval 153	Choose 17
Attack Dog 140	Climb 102
Auto Pilot 84	Coffee 79
A Woman 37	Compassion 7
Bad Choices 141	Compliments 42
Bad Habit 100	Contagious 111
Be and Eagle 27	Contaminated Heart 141
Being Right 22	Control Freaks 102
Believe 50	COVID-19 159
Be Restored 140	Credit Line 75

165

Criticize	97
Currency of Power	37
D	45
Dear Nurse	160
Death	99
Death is Welcomed	108
Delay Judgment	61
Desire	46
Destroy	56
Dicker	53
Dignity	43
Ditch the Baggage	25
Divide Your Love	87
Do & Done	77
Donald Trump	84
Don't Go	44
Do Something	71
Drama Queens	139
Drowning	135
Dummies	145
Eagle Scout	50
Ebb and Flow	81
Effort to Change	29
Eighty-Six	18
Elevate & Propel	19
Enemies	55
Everything	96
Extraordinary Life	142
Fault Finder	137
Fear Kills	48
Fear Not	58
Fisherman	126
Fish Out of Water	136
Fix It	83
Follow Me	68
Forgot	74
Friday	64
Friends & Family	35
Galatians 5:1	67
Get A Puppy	93
Get A Song	89
Get The Job Done	123
Getting & Giving	87
Giant Puzzle	95
Gift of Yourself	144
Gift To God	119
Glorious Miracle	71
God Gives	121
God is Love	15
God of Justice	20
God's Love & Guidance	16
God's Voice	113
Golden Goose	129
Good From Evil	133
Good Luck	82
Good Tenants	59
Good Things	124
Gossip	76
Grandchildren	73
Great Beauty	65
Great Woman	154
Grit & Glory	106

Grudge	21
Guilty & Regret	127
Guilty	125
Hair Day	7
Happiness	19
Happy Friday	97
Has Been	14
Haste	99
Have An Anchor	133
Heart Full	132
Hero	40
Higher Power	143
Hoarder	36
Hold On	114
Home	117
How to De-Stress	159
I Corinthians 13	34
Ignorance	20
Ignorance Can Kill	55
I Know I Am	113
Illness	8
Innocent	13
Inside Out	47
Intimidators	131
James 1:4	143
Journey	121
Keeping On	89
Language	90
Law of The Universe	29
Leave A Trail	78
Leave Me Alone	25
Lee-isms	91
Lick & A Promise	162
Life Manager	56
Life of Gratitude	86
Lifetime	94
Light & Sunshine	107
Like A Turtle	133
Limitations	112
Lived A Good Life	101
Lonely	111
Losing	54
Love	10
Love is Light	12
Love Lifted Me	115
Love & Peace	9
Love Thy Neighbor	30
Love Yourself	94
Luckier	83
Luke 7:4-7	33
Male Population	28
Mama Raised Me	92
Mama Said	30
Manager	53
Marriage	123
Masterpiece	24
Mental Abuse	41
Monday	62
More	85
More Blessings	143
More Than A Smoothie	73
Most Wonderful Book	164

Music Zone	149
My Illness	98
Never Give Up	15
Never Stop	151
No Matter	108
No More, No Less	88
No Secret	154
Not Perfect	28
Number One	31
Nursery	147
Office Hours	158
One Night Stand	69
One Track Mind	51
One Year	153
Opportunity Presents	139
Our Forests	103
Our Legacy	151
Our Mansion	110
Our Will	101
Own Client	57
Oyster	81
Pay The Dues	117
Peaceful Sleep	116
Peacemakers	150
Philemon	34
Philodendron	129
Pit of Depression	32
Positive Energy	78
Power to Feel	13
Precious Possession	11
Preparation	38
Pride	152
Promise	138
Proverbs 11:25	106
Read A Book	86
Recognize Your Soul	46
Recording	114
Relax & Enjoy	122
Resentments	79
Right or Wrong	32
Rise Up	104
Road Map	116
Romans 12:19	149
Roses	124
Rule of the Universe	66
Run The Race	82
Saints & Sinners	105
Saturday	64
Saving	45
Scorekeeper	148
Secret of Life	44
Seek Love	130
Self Respect	77
Senior Dance Camp	162
Short & Long Memory	24
Skeletons	31
Smile	90
Smug With Success	134
Sold Out	59
Song	36
Song for Chula	152
Sorry	27

Spring	155	Time	23
Stand On The Rock	136	Time To Live	146
Starbucks	14	Treasure	128
Stop Evil	134	True Image	47
Stop Thinking	52	Truth Wins	119
Story	57	Tuesday	62
Stream of Live	26	Ultimate Evil	16
Strongest Love	10	Unteachable	117
Success	17	Victim	49
Sunday	65	Victorious Over Grief	115
Teach Love	9	Voice of an Eagle	49
Tears	74	Wagging	126
Ten Commandments	72	Wednesday	63
Ten Foods For The Brain	163	Weight	80
The Bear	61	What If	85
The Best Love	8	What Is Grace?	131
The Dash	156	What You Want	68
The Facade	127	Whole Life	120
The Frame	144	Who You Are	128
The Game	57	Willing	96
The Great Life	41	Wonder	52
The Great Mechanic	17	Wonderful Things	147
The Right	59	Worthy	12
The Right Place	120	Wrong Turn	43
The Right Thing	104	You Are Free	118
The Saints	92	You Are Not	95
The Truth	135	Your Choice	33
Think	122	Zippidy	72
Think of You	91		
Three Words	70		
Thursday	63		

Notes

Notes

Notes

Notes

Made in the USA
Columbia, SC
09 June 2021